TAKE IT APART

CAR

By Chris Oxlade

Illustrated by Mike Grey

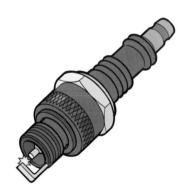
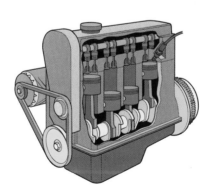

❤ Belitha Press

First Published in the UK in 1996 by
Belitha Press Limited, London House,
Great Eastern Wharf, Parkgate Road,
London SW11 4NQ

ISBN 1 85561 539 8

British Library in Cataloguing in Publication
Data for this book is available from the
British Library.

Printed in China

Editor: Jilly MacLeod
Designer: Guy Callaby
Illustrator: Mike Grey
Consultants: Robin Kerrod and
 Elizabeth Atkinson

Inside this Book

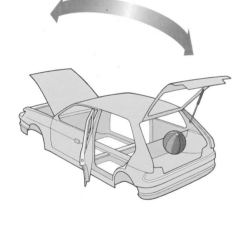

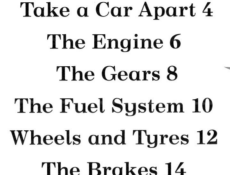

Take a Car Apart

- A car is made up of thousands of parts, big and small.

- The parts are made of different materials such as metal, plastic, rubber, glass and fabric. Sometimes leather and wood are used as well.

- All the parts are put together in a car factory.

- This book shows you the main parts of a car and how they all fit together.

exhaust pipe

seat

steering wheel

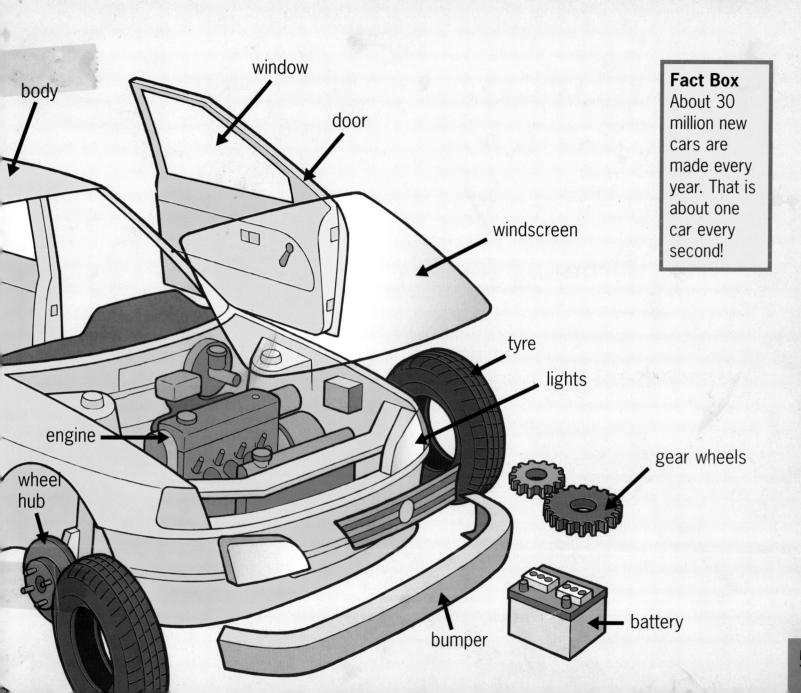

body

window

door

windscreen

tyre

lights

engine

gear wheels

wheel hub

bumper

battery

5

The Engine

- The engine makes the car move.

- Inside the engine are chambers called cylinders. Inside each cylinder is a piston which moves up and down.

- Fuel, such as petrol, is burned inside the cylinders to make the engine work.

- The driver presses the accelerator pedal with his foot to make the engine – and the car – go faster.

Spark plug
Spark plugs inside the engine make a spark, like a tiny flash of lightning, when electricity is passed through them.

spark

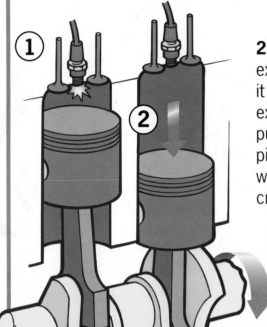

Up and down

1 Fuel inside the cylinder is set alight by an electric spark from a spark plug.

2 The fuel explodes when it burns. The explosion pushes the piston down, which turns a crankshaft.

3 As the crankshaft turns, it makes the wheels go round and the car moves.

crankshaft

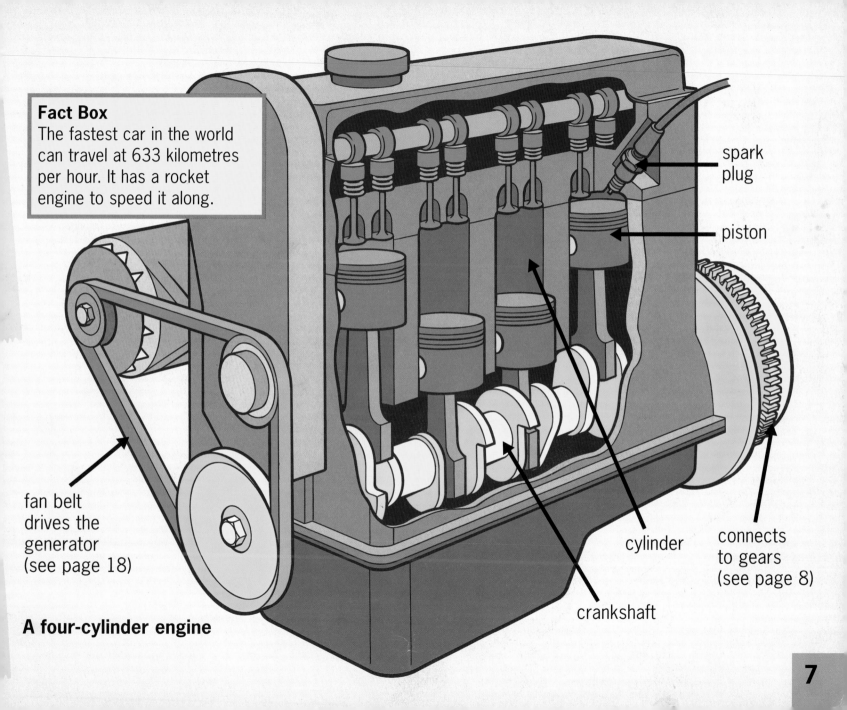

Fact Box
The fastest car in the world can travel at 633 kilometres per hour. It has a rocket engine to speed it along.

spark plug

piston

cylinder

connects to gears (see page 8)

crankshaft

fan belt drives the generator (see page 18)

A four-cylinder engine

The Gears

○ Most cars have four or five gears. They help the car to travel at different speeds.

○ Some gears are for starting off and driving slowly. Others are for driving fast or reversing (going backwards).

○ The gears are made up of lots of toothed wheels fixed to rods, or shafts.

○ When two gear wheels touch, the teeth fit together and one wheel turns the other.

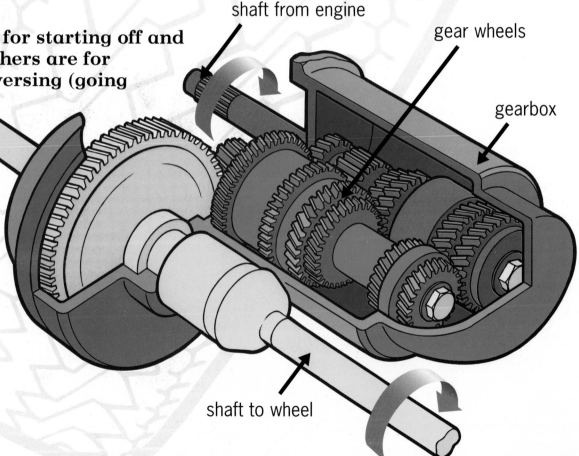

shaft from engine

gear wheels

gearbox

shaft to wheel

Fast and slow

The gear wheels are different sizes. Big gear wheels turn the shaft to the wheels faster than small gear wheels.

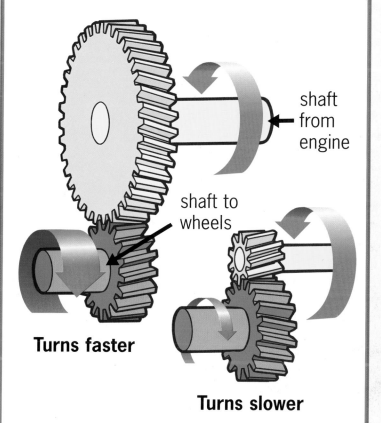

shaft from engine

shaft to wheels

Turns faster

Turns slower

Changing gear

In some cars, the gears change automatically. The gear lever is used for driving forwards (D), reversing (R) and parking (P). N is for neutral, meaning no gear.

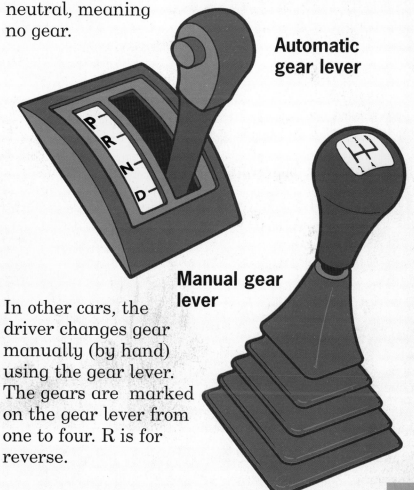

Automatic gear lever

Manual gear lever

In other cars, the driver changes gear manually (by hand) using the gear lever. The gears are marked on the gear lever from one to four. R is for reverse.

The Fuel System

⊘ **Fuel for the engine is stored in the fuel tank.**

⊘ **When fuel explodes in the engine it makes waste gases.**

◉ **The waste, or exhaust, gases go along the exhaust pipe and out of the car into the air.**

Fact Box
Some large cars have such big, powerful engines that they need two or more exhaust pipes to get rid of all the waste gases.

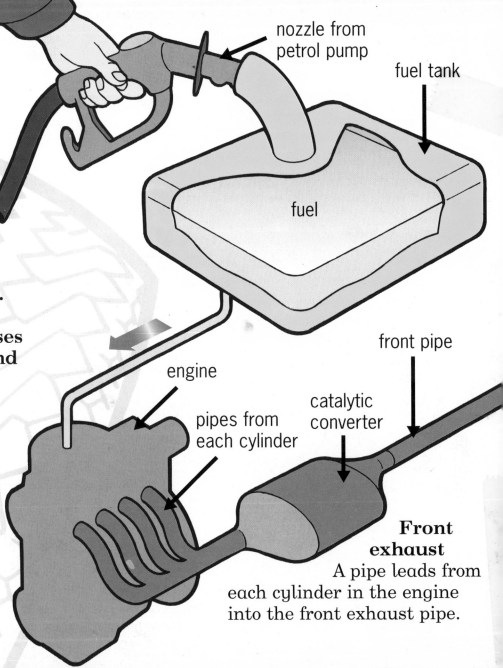

nozzle from petrol pump

fuel tank

fuel

front pipe

engine

pipes from each cylinder

catalytic converter

Front exhaust
A pipe leads from each cylinder in the engine into the front exhaust pipe.

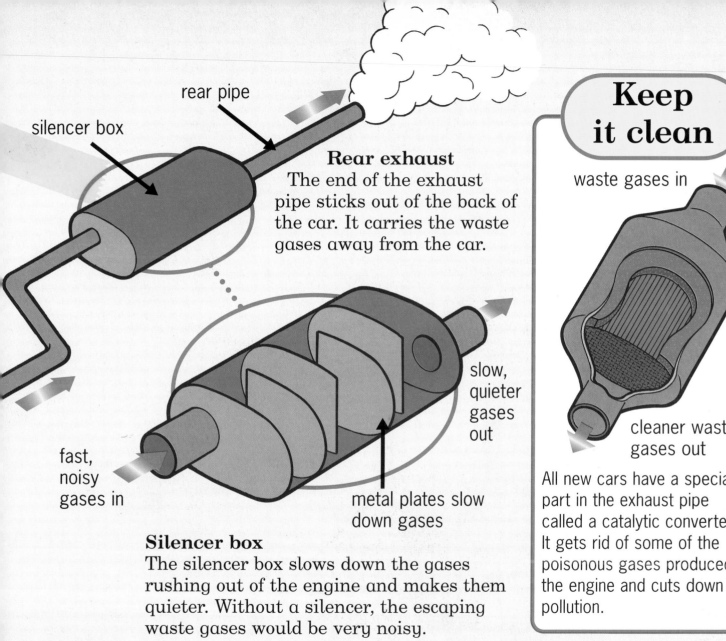

silencer box

rear pipe

Rear exhaust
The end of the exhaust pipe sticks out of the back of the car. It carries the waste gases away from the car.

fast, noisy gases in

slow, quieter gases out

metal plates slow down gases

Silencer box
The silencer box slows down the gases rushing out of the engine and makes them quieter. Without a silencer, the escaping waste gases would be very noisy.

waste gases in

cleaner waste gases out

All new cars have a special part in the exhaust pipe called a catalytic converter. It gets rid of some of the poisonous gases produced in the engine and cuts down pollution.

Wheels and Tyres

⊘ **Most cars have four wheels, two at the front and two at the back.**

⊘ **The wheels are covered with tyres which help to grip the road and give a smooth ride.**

⊘ **The tyres are lined with layers of thick fabric to make them strong.**

Fact Box
Wheels were invented more than 5 000 years ago. The first wheels were of solid wood.

tyre

hub cap

tread

nuts and bolts

wheel

fabric lining

Parts of a wheel

Hub cap
The hub cap covers the nuts and bolts that fix the wheel to the car.

Tyre
The tyre is made of rubber and filled with air. It is the only part of the car to touch the ground.

Wheel
The wheel rim holds the tyre in place. It is made of steel or aluminium.

Spring
A spring lets the wheel move up and down slightly. This gives a smooth ride on bumpy roads.

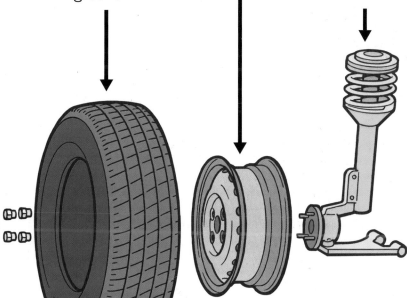

Tread carefully!
The patterns on tyres are called treads. They help the car to grip the road in wet weather.

The Brakes

● Brakes are used to slow down the car and make it stop.

● Each wheel has its own brake. The front wheels have 'disc' brakes, and the back wheels usually have 'drum' brakes.

● The driver presses the brake pedal to put on the brakes.

● The brake pedal is connected to the brakes by pipes filled with a liquid called brake fluid.

Fact Box
Racing car brakes get so hot that they glow red. Cool air is pumped around them to stop them melting.

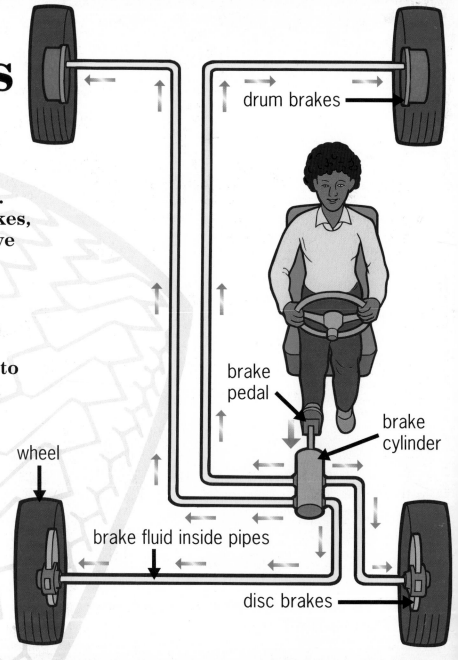

drum brakes

brake pedal

brake cylinder

wheel

brake fluid inside pipes

disc brakes

Putting on the brakes

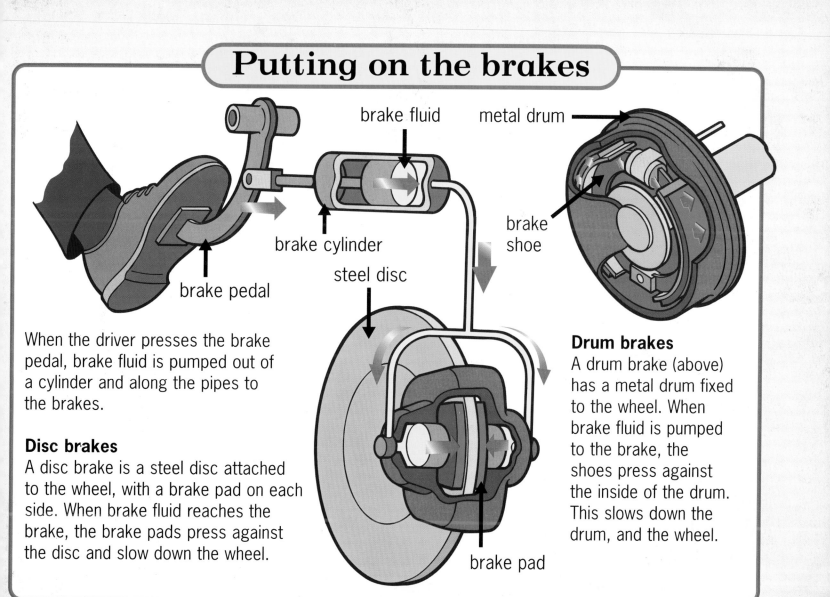

brake fluid

metal drum

brake cylinder

steel disc

brake shoe

brake pedal

brake pad

When the driver presses the brake pedal, brake fluid is pumped out of a cylinder and along the pipes to the brakes.

Disc brakes

A disc brake is a steel disc attached to the wheel, with a brake pad on each side. When brake fluid reaches the brake, the brake pads press against the disc and slow down the wheel.

Drum brakes

A drum brake (above) has a metal drum fixed to the wheel. When brake fluid is pumped to the brake, the shoes press against the inside of the drum. This slows down the drum, and the wheel.

Steering

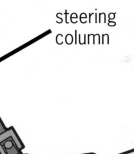

⊘ The driver turns the steering wheel to make the car turn left or right.

⊘ The steering wheel turns the front wheels from side to side.

⊘ In some cars, fluid in a system of pipes is used to help turn the wheels. This is called 'power-assisted steering'. It makes it easier for the driver to steer the car.

steering wheel

steering column

wheel

Fact Box
The first cars had no steering wheel. Instead, the driver steered by moving a wooden stick, called a tiller, from side to side.

16

How the steering works

Steering column

The steering wheel is joined to the top of the steering column. When the driver turns the wheel, the steering column turns too.

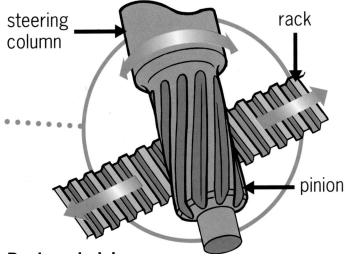

steering column

rack

pinion

Rack and pinion

At the bottom of the steering column is a gear wheel called a pinion. When it turns, it makes a long bar called a rack move from side to side. This makes the wheels turn.

Turning left

When the steering wheel is turned to the left, the rack moves to the right and turns the front wheels to the left.

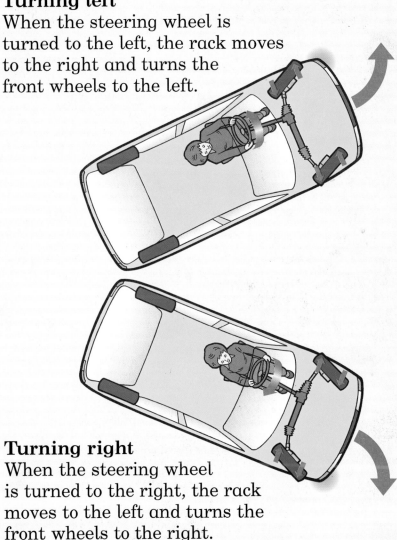

Turning right

When the steering wheel is turned to the right, the rack moves to the left and turns the front wheels to the right.

Lights and Electrics

● A car has four main groups of lights, two groups at the front and two at the back.

● The lights are powered by electricity from a machine called a generator.

● Electricity is also used to power the spark plugs, radio, heater and wipers.

Making electricity

Generator
When the engine is running (turned on), it turns round the generator. As it spins, the generator makes electricity.

Battery
When the engine is turned off, electricity for the lights comes from the battery. The battery is recharged by the generator.

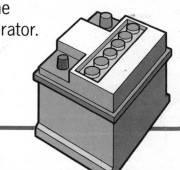

Parts of a headlight

reflector gathers light from bulb into a narrow beam

bulb produces light

lens shines beam in the right direction

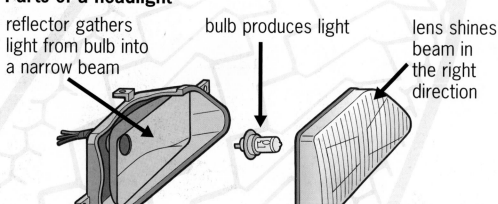

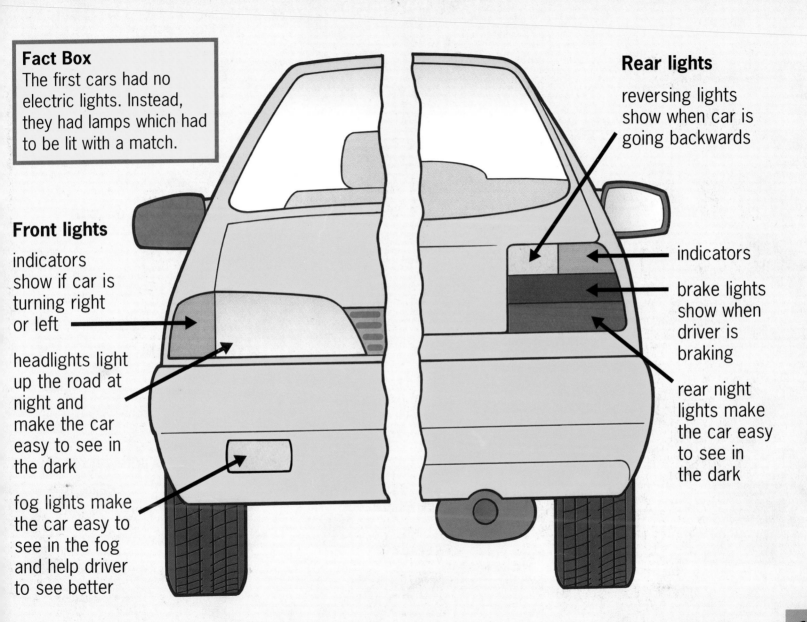

Fact Box
The first cars had no
electric lights. Instead,
they had lamps which had
to be lit with a match.

Rear lights

reversing lights
show when car is
going backwards

Front lights

indicators
show if car is
turning right
or left

indicators

headlights light
up the road at
night and
make the car
easy to see in
the dark

brake lights
show when
driver is
braking

rear night
lights make
the car easy
to see in
the dark

fog lights make
the car easy to
see in the fog
and help driver
to see better

Inside the Car

⊘ **There are comfortable seats inside the car, firmly fixed to the floor.**

⊘ **The seats can be adjusted to suit tall or short people.**

⊘ **Mirrors are fitted to let the driver see what is on the road behind.**

⊘ **Seat belts, headrests and sometimes airbags are fitted to keep the driver and passengers safe in an accident.**

Mirrors

The driver looks in a mirror above the windscreen to see what is behind. Mirrors fitted to the wings outside give a wider view.

Handles and armrests

On the inside of the doors there are handles to open and close the doors and windows, plus an armrest to lean on.

Carpets and covers

There is carpet on the floor and soft fabric covering the seats. In expensive cars, the seats may be covered in leather.

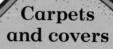

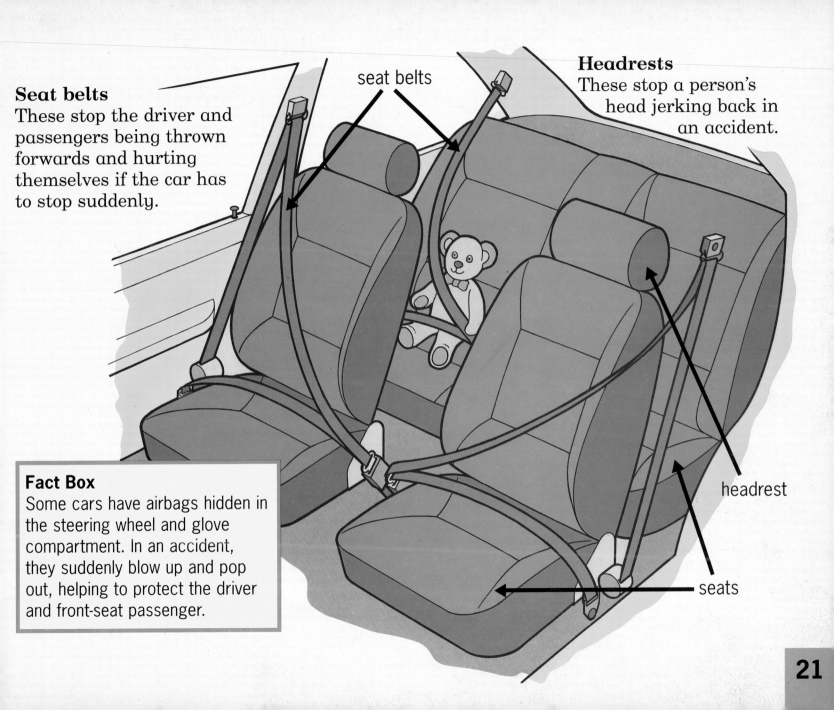

Seat belts
These stop the driver and passengers being thrown forwards and hurting themselves if the car has to stop suddenly.

seat belts

Headrests
These stop a person's head jerking back in an accident.

Fact Box
Some cars have airbags hidden in the steering wheel and glove compartment. In an accident, they suddenly blow up and pop out, helping to protect the driver and front-seat passenger.

headrest

seats

21

The Dashboard

● The dashboard is a display of lights, measuring instruments and switches.

● Measuring instruments, or gauges, give the driver information about the car.

● One set of switches controls the heating inside the car.

● Warning lights come on to warn the driver if something is wrong.

● There are also switches on the steering column to control the lights, indicators and windscreen wipers.

Fact Box
Some modern cars have speaking dashboards. They tell people to fasten their seat belt and close their door properly.

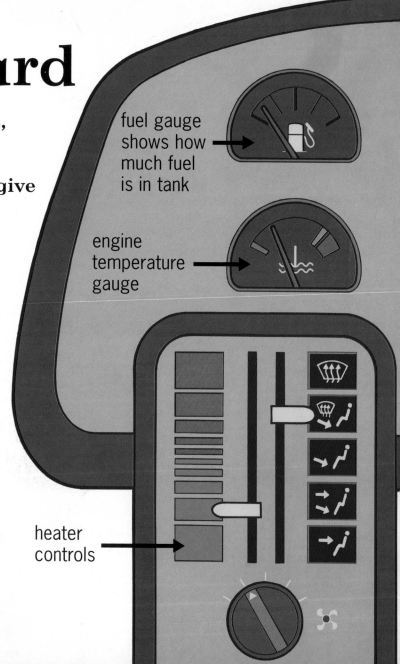

fuel gauge shows how much fuel is in tank

engine temperature gauge

heater controls

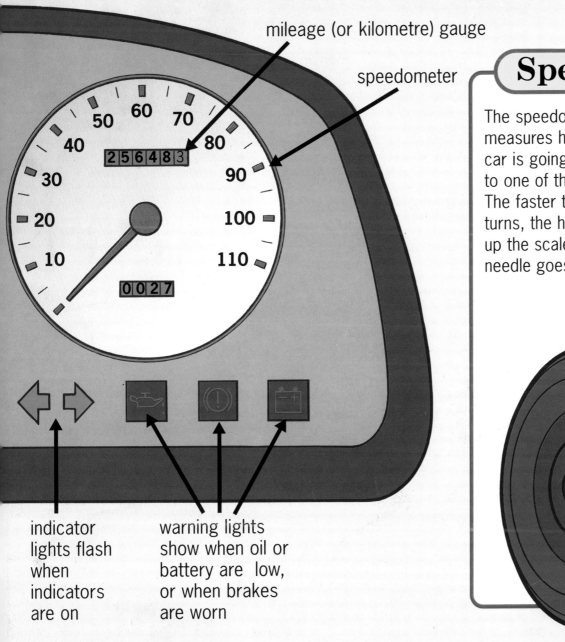

mileage (or kilometre) gauge

speedometer

256483

0027

indicator lights flash when indicators are on

warning lights show when oil or battery are low, or when brakes are worn

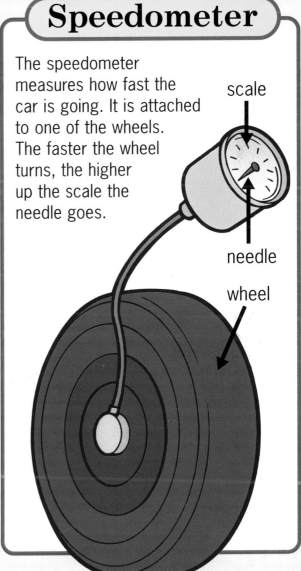

Speedometer

The speedometer measures how fast the car is going. It is attached to one of the wheels. The faster the wheel turns, the higher up the scale the needle goes.

scale

needle

wheel

The Bodywork

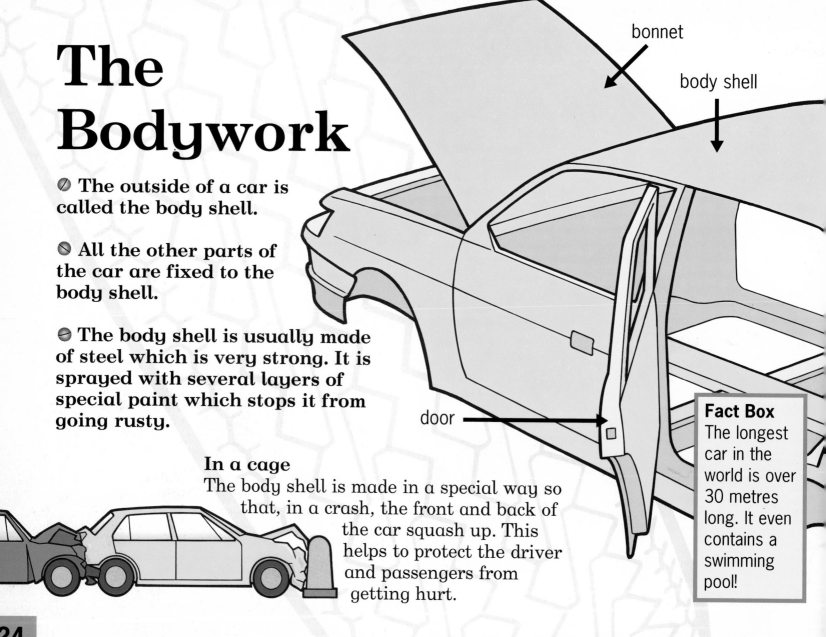

🔩 The outside of a car is called the body shell.

🔩 All the other parts of the car are fixed to the body shell.

🔩 The body shell is usually made of steel which is very strong. It is sprayed with several layers of special paint which stops it from going rusty.

In a cage
The body shell is made in a special way so that, in a crash, the front and back of the car squash up. This helps to protect the driver and passengers from getting hurt.

bonnet

body shell

door

Fact Box
The longest car in the world is over 30 metres long. It even contains a swimming pool!

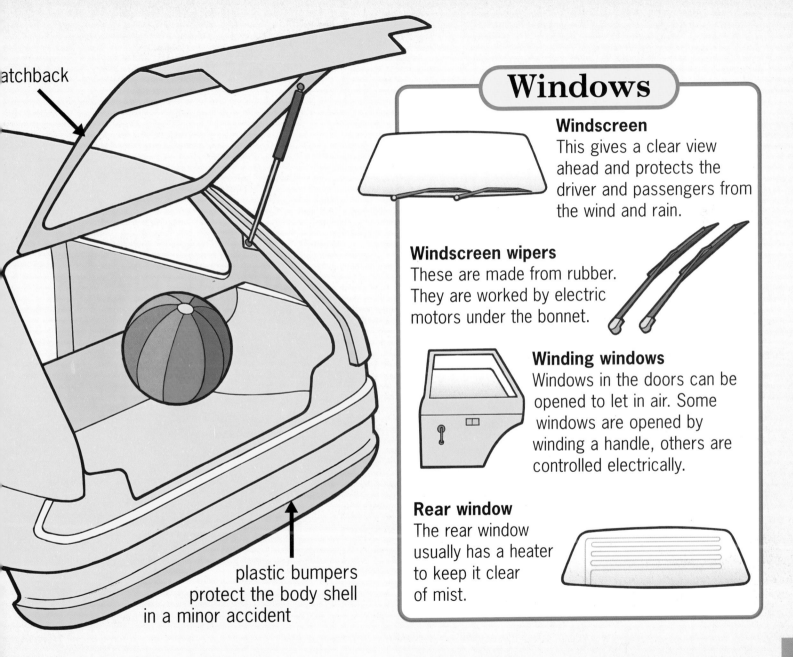

atchback

plastic bumpers
protect the body shell
in a minor accident

Windows

Windscreen
This gives a clear view
ahead and protects the
driver and passengers from
the wind and rain.

Windscreen wipers
These are made from rubber.
They are worked by electric
motors under the bonnet.

Winding windows
Windows in the doors can be
opened to let in air. Some
windows are opened by
winding a handle, others are
controlled electrically.

Rear window
The rear window
usually has a heater
to keep it clear
of mist.

How a Car is Built

- Cars are made on a production line in a factory.

- Different parts are added as the car moves along the production line.

- Some of the jobs on the line are done by robots.

- Some parts, such as the engine, are made on their own production line before being fixed to the car.

Making the body shell
Metal sheets are pressed into shape and welded together to form the shell.

Painting the body shell
The shell is dipped in a huge bath of chemicals to stop it rusting. Then it is painted.

Adding the engine
The engine is put in the bonnet and fixed into place. Other parts are also added.

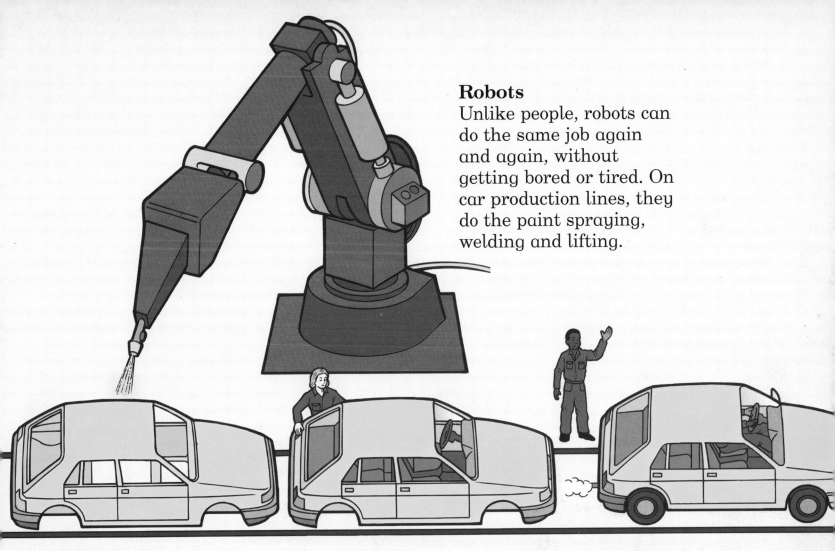

Robots
Unlike people, robots can do the same job again and again, without getting bored or tired. On car production lines, they do the paint spraying, welding and lifting.

Doors and bonnet
The doors and bonnet are painted separately. Then they are fixed to the body.

Seats and fittings
The carpets and seats, door knobs and handles, and seat belts are added next.

Finishing off
Finally, the windows and wheels are added. Then the car is driven off to be tested.

Special Parts

⬤ Some cars are built for special jobs.

⬤ They have different parts from normal cars.

⬤ You can see some of these special parts on this spread.

Flashing lights
Emergency vehicles, such as police cars and ambulances, have flashing lights on the roof to warn other drivers to clear the road.

Parachutes
Drag racing cars, or dragsters, go so fast that they need a parachute to help slow them down again.

Wings

Racing cars have a wing-like shape on the back. This pushes the back of the car down so that the car grips the road better when it is going fast.

Roll bars

Rally cars have bars inside them which protect the driver and co-driver if the car rolls over.

Soft-tops

Some cars have a soft roof which can be folded down in sunny weather. These cars are called convertibles or soft-tops.

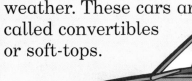

Wheelchair lift

Cars can be fitted with a special mechanism that lifts a wheelchair and its passenger inside the car. The wheelchair then locks firmly in place and acts as a car seat.

Useful Terms

airbag A large plastic bag, like a balloon, that inflates (fills with air) very quickly in an accident to protect the driver or passenger from being thrown forwards.

battery A device that stores electricity so that it can be used later. Car batteries are much heavier and last much longer than torch batteries.

bumper A piece of metal or plastic at the front or back of a car body that stops the car getting damaged in a minor accident.

catalytic converter A metal box in the exhaust pipe that gets rid of some of the poisonous gases from the engine and helps to cut down pollution.

convertible A car with a roof that folds down so that the passengers are in the open air.

crankshaft The shaft turned by the pistons in a car's engine. It goes into the gearbox.

cylinder A hole in the engine – the shape of a fizzy drink can – where fuel burns. Pistons move up and down inside the cylinders. There are also cylinders in the brakes. Pistons move out of them to make the brakes work.

dashboard The panel of switches, lights and dials in front of the driver.

disc brake A brake that slows down the car by forcing two pads against a metal disc fixed to the wheel.

drum brake A brake that slows down the car by pressing pads on to the inside of a metal drum fixed to the wheel.

exhaust A long pipe that takes waste gases from the engine and releases them into the air behind the car.

four-cylinder engine
An engine with four cylinders. Some engines have six, eight or even twelve cylinders to make them more powerful.

fuel A liquid that is burned inside the engine to make the engine work and the car move. It is stored in a fuel tank.

gears A set of gear wheels (metal discs with teeth around the rim) that lets the car go faster or slower, or forwards or backwards.

indicators Flashing lights at each corner of a car that tell other drivers which way the car is going to turn.

lights These are used to light up the road at night and let other drivers see the car, and to show when the car is turning or reversing. There are also warning lights on the dashboard.

piston A piece of metal that moves up and down inside the cylinder of an engine. As it moves, it turns the engine's crankshaft.

power-assisted steering
Steering that helps the driver by making the steering wheel easier to turn.

production line The line of machines and workers in a factory along which a car moves as it is being built.

rocket engine An engine that works by shooting out a stream of hot gases. Rocket engines are usually used for missiles and spacecraft.

seat belt A long belt made of fabric that holds the driver and passengers in their seats. It stops them being thrown about inside the car in a accident.

silencer box A metal box that is part of a car's exhaust pipe. It makes the engine much less noisy.

tyre A rubber cover on the outside of a wheel. It helps the car grip the road, and makes the ride less bumpy.

windscreen The large window at the front of the car. It protects the driver and passengers from the wind and rain.

Index

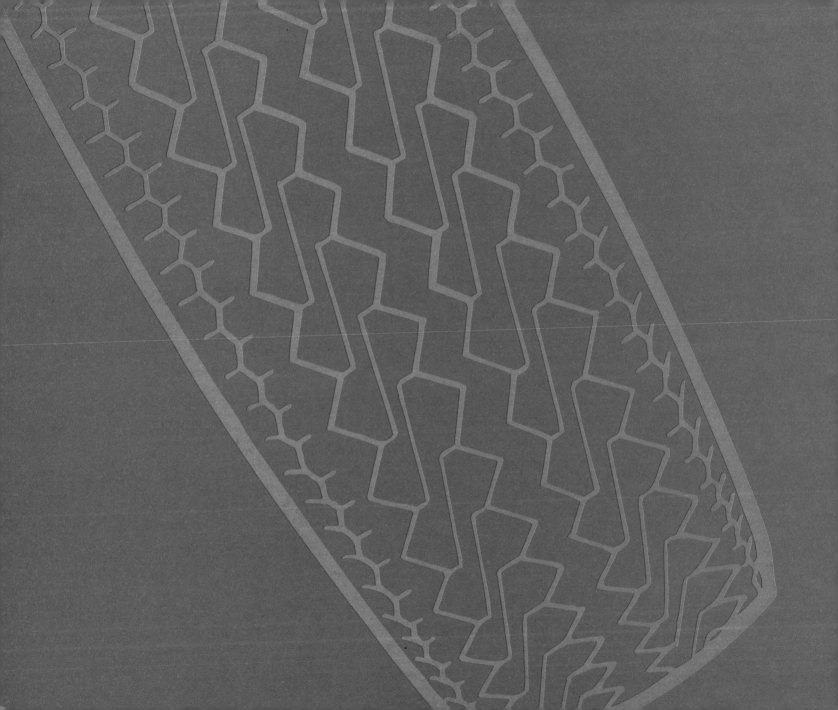